Non-Techie to Tech in 30 Days

Adebola Sanni

Published by Adebola Sanni, 2023.

NON-TECHIE TO TECH IN 30 DAYS

First edition. May 6, 2023.

Written by Adebola Sanni.

This e-book is dedicated to **my husband**, who has been my constant support and a source of inspiration throughout our beautiful years together.

To my lovely daughters, who have always been my biggest fans and never ceased to root for mummy.

And to my dear friend, IK, who has always encouraged me to teach what I know and has been instrumental in bringing this e-book to reality.

Thank you all for your unwavering support and belief in me.

Introduction

Are you a non-techie who wants to work in technology but lacks the necessary technical skills? Are you overwhelmed by the seemingly complex world of technology and unsure where to begin? If so, **"Non-Techie to Tech in 30 Days"** is the book to turn your tech dreams into reality.

The demand for tech talent is constantly increasing in today's fast-paced digital world. You don't have to be a coding prodigy or a computer science graduate to work in technology. This book is intended for non-techies like you who want to work in technology but lack traditional technical skills. You can leverage your existing skills and experience to transition to a new career with the right mindset, strategy, and determination to achieve a fulfilling income.

Whether you're a career changer, a recent graduate, a stay-at-home parent, or anyone looking to make a career change, this book is the ultimate companion to help you confidently embark on your tech journey.

This book, written in an understandable and jargon-free language, covers everything you need to know to transition to a tech career. This book covers everything from understanding the tech industry and job market to identifying your transferable skills and developing a learning plan for tech skills, with links to mastering resume writing, job search strategies, and interview techniques.

You'll also learn how to build your tech brand, navigate online resources for learning tech skills, find and join tech communities and networks, and negotiate job offers and compensation in the tech industry.

However, this book goes beyond simply providing information and tips. It goes above and beyond by providing real-life success stories of non-techies who have made it big in the tech industry. The stories of people who successfully transitioned from non-tech backgrounds to thriving tech careers will inspire and motivate you, proving that you can achieve your tech dreams even if you don't have a traditional tech background.

Chapter I

Understanding the Tech Industry

The tech industry is one of the world's most dynamic and rapidly evolving industries. From software development to data analytics, the tech industry offers a vast array of products, services, and technologies designed to improve people's lives and work. In this section, we'll delve deeper into the tech industry and explore its various aspects in greater detail.

Overview of the Tech Industry

The technology industry is a rapidly growing sector encompassing a wide range of companies and organisations that produce and market products and services based on technological advancements. It contains hardware, software, telecommunications companies, and firms that provide technology-related services, such as consulting, support, and training.

One of the critical aspects of the technology industry is innovation, with companies constantly striving to create new products and services that offer improved functionality and increased customer convenience. This has resulted in a rapidly evolving industry characterised by rapid changes and advancements and intense competition among companies.

Hardware companies in the technology industry produce a wide range of products, from personal computers and mobile devices to servers and networking equipment. These companies are responsible for developing and manufacturing the physical components that make up technology systems and devices, as well as the accompanying software and firmware.

On the other hand, software companies specialise in developing and marketing software products and services designed to run on hardware systems. This includes everything from operating systems and productivity software to video games and mobile applications.

Telecommunications companies provide the underlying infrastructure and services for communication and data transmission, such as phone and internet services. They also play a vital role in developing and implementing new communication technologies, such as 5G and the Internet of Things (IoT). The technology industry is also responsible for driving much of the economic growth and development in recent decades, with companies in the sector creating high-paying jobs and contributing significantly to overall economic growth. As technology continues to advance and play an increasingly important role in our lives, it is expected that the technology industry will continue to play a significant role in shaping the future.

Types of Tech Jobs

The tech industry offers diverse job opportunities for individuals with various skills and interests. Some of the most common tech jobs include

- **Quality Assurance:** Quality Assurance (QA) plays a critical role in the technology industry, as it is responsible for ensuring that products and services meet customer requirements and are of high quality. QA professionals are responsible for testing products and services to identify defects or issues and working with development teams to resolve them. They also develop and implement testing plans and write test cases and scripts to ensure that products are thoroughly tested before they are released to customers.

● **Business Analysis:** A Business Analyst (BA) is a professional who works with organisations to identify and solve business problems using technology and process improvement techniques. BAs are responsible for gathering and analysing business requirements, developing solutions, and communicating those solutions to the relevant stakeholders. They work closely with stakeholders such as stakeholders, project managers and development teams to ensure that technology solutions align with the needs of the business and are delivered on time and within budget.

● **Solution Architects:** Solution Architects are responsible for designing and developing organisational technology solutions. They work with stakeholders to understand the organisation's business requirements and objectives and use that information to develop a high-level architecture for a technology solution. Solution Architects then work with development teams to ensure that the technology solution is built to meet the specified requirements and is aligned with the organisation's technology roadmap.

- **Software Developer:** Software developers are responsible for designing, developing, and testing software programs and applications for various platforms and devices. They work with various programming languages and technologies to create functional and user-friendly programs.

- **Data Analyst:** Data analysts are responsible for analysing large amounts of data and using the insights they gain to inform decision-making and solve complex problems. They work with data from various sources and use statistical methods and data visualisation tools to uncover patterns and trends.

- **Project Manager:** Project managers are responsible for managing projects and coordinating the work of a team to ensure that projects are completed on time and within budget. They work with stakeholders, team members, and customers to plan, organise, and execute projects.

- **Customer Support Specialist**: Customer support specialists are responsible for assisting customers with technical issues and helping to resolve any problems they may encounter. They work with customers via phone, email, or live chat to provide technical support and troubleshoot issues.

Key Skills in the Tech Industry

To be successful in the tech industry, individuals need to possess a combination of technical and non-technical (soft) skills. Some of the most important skills for a tech career include

- **Problem-solving:** Problem-solving is a critical skill in the tech industry, where challenges are a daily occurrence. Software developers, data analysts, and other tech professionals must be able to identify problems, find solutions, and implement them effectively.

- **Empathy:** Empathy is a crucial skill for success in the technology industry as it enables individuals to understand and connect with the needs, feelings, and perspectives of others. Empathy helps individuals to build stronger relationships with customers, stakeholders, and team members and to understand their needs better, which can lead to more successful outcomes. In the technology industry, individuals with strong empathy skills can often develop more effective and user-friendly technology solutions and build stronger, more collaborative teams.

- **Storytelling:** Storytelling is another important skill in the technology industry, as it allows individuals to communicate complex ideas and information in a way that is easy to understand and engaging. By using stories and anecdotes, individuals can make technical concepts accessible and interesting to a wider audience and help build buy-in and support for their ideas and solutions.

• **Time management:** Time management is also a critical skill in the technology industry, as technology projects and initiatives often have tight deadlines and require individuals to be able to prioritise and manage their time effectively. Individuals with strong time management skills can stay organised and focused and meet their deadlines, which can be critical for the success of technology projects.

• **Collaboration:** Collaboration is another important skill in the technology industry, as technology projects often involve cross-functional teams and require individuals to work closely with others to achieve their goals. Individuals with strong collaboration skills can work effectively with others, communicate their ideas and perspectives, and build consensus, which can lead to better outcomes and more successful technology projects.

• **Interpersonal:** Interpersonal skills are essential for success in the technology industry, as technology professionals often work in teams and must interact with a wide range of stakeholders, including customers, stakeholders, and team members. Interpersonal skills include communicating effectively verbally and in writing and building and maintaining positive relationships with others. In the technology industry, it is also important for individuals to be able to listen to and understand the needs and perspectives of others and to be able to work collaboratively to resolve conflicts.

● **Teamwork:** Teamwork is another key skill for success in the technology industry, as most technology projects are completed by teams of individuals working together to achieve common goals. Teamwork skills include the ability to work effectively with others, to share information and ideas, and to provide support and assistance to team members. In the technology industry, it is also important for individuals to be able to lead and manage teams, as well as to be able to work effectively in a team environment.

● **Critical thinking:** Critical thinking is a critical skill for success in the technology industry, as technology professionals are often faced with complex and challenging problems that require creative and innovative solutions. Critical thinking skills include analysing and evaluating information, identifying patterns and relationships, and developing and implementing effective solutions. In the technology industry, it is also important for individuals to be able to think critically about technology trends and developments and to be able to anticipate and respond to changes in the technology landscape.

● **Communication:** Effective communication is essential in the tech industry, where individuals often work in teams and must communicate with customers, stakeholders, and team members. Individuals need to be able to articulate complex technical concepts clearly and concisely and listen effectively to the needs and concerns of others.

● **Adaptability:** The tech industry is constantly changing, and individuals need to be adaptable and open to new technologies to stay ahead of the curve. This requires a willingness to learn, an eagerness to embrace change, and an ability to adapt to new tools and technologies as they become available.

● **Attention to detail:** A high level of attention to detail is necessary for the tech industry, where small errors can have significant consequences. Individuals need to be meticulous in their work and have an eye for detail to ensure that software and systems function as intended.

Career Paths in Tech

The tech industry offers various career paths, from entry-level positions to senior leadership roles. Some individuals start their careers in entry-level positions and work their way up, while others may begin as freelancers or entrepreneurs and build their businesses. Some common career paths in tech include

● **Junior Developer:** A starting position for individuals with other soft skills, a junior developer is responsible for working on small aspects of software development projects under the supervision of more experienced developers.

● **IT Sales and Marketing:** IT Sales and Marketing professionals are responsible for promoting and selling technology products and services to customers. They work with stakeholders to understand their needs and use that information to develop and implement marketing strategies that will help drive sales. IT Sales and Marketing professionals also work closely with technical teams to ensure that products and services meet customer requirements and are of high quality.

● **Network Engineer:** Network Engineers are responsible for designing, implementing, and maintaining computer networks. They work with stakeholders to understand their network requirements and use that information to design and implement network solutions that meet their needs. Network Engineers also work to ensure that networks are secure and perform optimally, and they may be responsible for troubleshooting and resolving network issues.

● **QA/Tester:** QA/Testers are responsible for testing technology products and services to ensure that they meet customer requirements and are of high quality. They work with development teams to identify defects and issues, develop and implement testing plans and write test cases to ensure that products are thoroughly tested before they are released to customers.

● **Technical Writer:** Technical Writers are responsible for creating technical documentation that is clear, accurate, and easy to understand. They work with development teams to gather information about technology products and services and use that information to create user manuals, installation guides, and other technical documents. Technical Writers also ensure that documentation is updated and maintained as technology evolves.

- **Data Scientist:** Data scientists are responsible for designing and implementing complex data analytics projects, and they typically have advanced training in mathematics, statistics, and computer science. They use advanced statistical techniques to analyse data and extract insights that can inform decision-making and drive innovation.

- **Product Manager:** Product managers are responsible for leading the development of products from concept to launch. They work with cross-functional teams of developers, designers, and other stakeholders to define the product roadmap, prioritise features, and manage the product launch process.

- **DevOps Engineer:** DevOps engineers automate the software development and deployment process. They work with developers and operations teams to create efficient workflows that streamline the development and deployment process, reduce errors, and improve overall quality.

● **Cybersecurity Specialist:** Cybersecurity specialists protect an organisation's digital assets and infrastructure from cyber threats. They use technical and non-soft skills to implement and manage security controls, respond to security incidents, and advise organisations on best practices for cyber security.

● **IT Support Specialist:** IT support specialists are responsible for providing technical support to users and resolving technical issues. They work with users to diagnose and resolve technical problems, provide training and support, and maintain documentation and knowledge databases.

Benefits of a Career in Tech

A career in the tech industry can offer many benefits, including:

● **High demand for skilled professionals**: The tech industry is increasing, and there is a high demand for skilled professionals. This demand is expected to continue in the coming years, providing individuals with a wide range of job opportunities and career advancement possibilities.

● **High salaries:** Tech jobs tend to pay well, with many positions offering salaries significantly higher than the national average. This is due in part to the high level of technical expertise required for many positions in the tech industry and the high demand for skilled professionals.

- **Opportunity to work with cutting-edge technologies:** The tech industry is at the forefront of innovation, and individuals who work in tech have the opportunity to work with the latest and most remarkable technologies. This can be especially exciting for those who enjoy learning and exploring new technologies.

- **Flexible work arrangements:** Many tech companies offer flexible work arrangements, such as remote work and flexible schedules, that can provide employees with a greater work-life balance. This can be especially beneficial for those who value flexibility and autonomy in their work.

- **A dynamic and challenging work environment:** The tech industry constantly evolves and offers a dynamic and challenging work environment. Individuals who work in tech can often take on new and exciting projects, solve complex problems, and collaborate with diverse professionals.

The tech industry is an exciting and dynamic field that is constantly evolving. This means that individuals pursuing a career in tech can expect to continuously learn and grow as they work with the latest technologies and develop new skills.

A critical aspect of the tech industry is collaboration. Many tech jobs require individuals to work with cross-functional teams, including developers, designers, product managers, and business stakeholders. This collaborative approach to work can foster innovation, as individuals bring different perspectives and expertise to the table.

For individuals interested in positively impacting the world, a career in the tech industry can offer a unique opportunity to do so. Tech companies are using technology to solve complex problems and improve people's lives, and individuals who work in tech have the opportunity to contribute to these efforts. For example, data scientists may use advanced analytical techniques to help healthcare organisations better understand disease outbreaks and improve public health. Developers may use their skills to create innovative products that make it easier for people to access essential services, such as healthcare and education. And cybersecurity specialists may help protect organisations and individuals from cyber threats, ensuring that sensitive information and personal data are kept secure.

Ultimately, a career in the tech industry can offer individuals the opportunity to be part of a dynamic and evolving field, to work with cutting-edge technologies, to collaborate with others, and to make a positive impact on the world. Whether you are interested in software development, data science, project management, cybersecurity, or another area of tech, a rewarding career path is waiting for you.

For individuals who are just starting in tech, several resources and training programs are available to help you build your skills and gain experience. For example, many tech companies offer internships and entry-level positions for individuals just starting in the field. Additionally, it is advisable to possess soft skills to work in the tech industry. However, acquiring tech skills through online learning resources such as coding boot camps and online courses can be advantageous and boost an individual's chances of success in the industry.

Assessment

- Take a moment to research job postings in the tech industry and identify the key skills and qualifications that employers are looking for in your desired role.

- How can you develop these skills and qualifications to become a stronger candidate?
- What types of businesses and organisations make up the tech industry?
- Why might someone be interested in pursuing a career in the tech industry?
- What key trends or innovations in the tech industry that you think will significantly impact in the next few years?

Chapter II

The fundamental understanding of the tech industry, including its various types of businesses and organisations, roles, and opportunities

The tech industry is a broad and diverse field that encompasses a wide range of companies and organisations and many different types of jobs and roles. Understanding the basic structure of the tech industry and the different types of companies and organisations that make it up can help individuals determine which types of roles and opportunities might be the best fit for them.

One of the critical features of the tech industry is that it constantly evolves and grows. This means there are always new technologies being developed and new types of companies emerging. Some key companies that make up the tech industry include

Software Development Companies, which specialise in developing software products for various industries and applications. This can include everything from enterprise software for large corporations to consumer-focused applications for mobile devices.

- Microsoft

- Amazon Web Services

- Google

- Oracle

- Salesforce

Data Analytics and AI Companies: These companies specialise in collecting, analysing, and interpreting data to help organisations make informed decisions. They may use machine learning algorithms and other advanced analytics techniques to help organisations better understand their customers, predict future trends, and optimise their operations.

- IBM

- Palantir Technologies

- SAS Institute

- Tableau

- Splunk

Cybersecurity Companies: These companies help protect organisations and individuals from cyber threats, such as hacking and data breaches. They may provide a range of services, including network security, data encryption, and threat intelligence.

- Symantec

- McAfee

- Trend Micro

- Check Point

- Cisco Systems

Hardware and Device Companies: These companies specialise in developing and manufacturing physical devices and products, such as smartphones, laptops, and wearable devices.

- Apple

- Samsung

- HP

- Dell

- Lenovo

Internet and Online Services Companies: These companies provide a wide range of online services, including social media, e-commerce, and cloud computing.

- Facebook

- Google

- Amazon

- Netflix

- Twitter

In addition to these types of companies, many different types of organisations play essential roles in the tech industry. For example, research institutions, universities, and think tanks conduct research and development in critical technology areas. There are also trade associations, industry groups, and advocacy organisations that work to promote the interests of the tech industry and to support the growth and development of technology companies.

There are many different paths that individuals can pursue in the various roles and opportunities available within the tech industry. Some of the most common roles in the tech industry include

- **Software Developers:** These individuals are responsible for designing, coding, and testing software applications. They may specialise in a particular programming language or type of software, such as mobile applications or enterprise software.

- **Business Intelligence Specialist:** A Business Intelligence (BI) Specialist is a professional responsible for using data and analysis to support and inform business decision-making. BI Specialists work with stakeholders to understand their data needs and to design and implement solutions that will meet those needs.

- **Project Managers:** These individuals are responsible for overseeing the planning, execution, and delivery of technology projects. They may work with cross-functional teams, including developers, designers, and business stakeholders, to ensure that projects are completed on time and within budget.

- **Business Analyst**: These individuals help organisations understand their operations and identify opportunities for improvement. They may gather and analyse data, create reports and presentations, and work with stakeholders to implement changes.

- **Cybersecurity Specialists:** These individuals are responsible for protecting organisations and individuals from cyber threats, such as hacking and data breaches. They may work in various areas, including network security, threat intelligence, and incident response.

- **Product Managers:** These individuals are responsible for defining and launching new products. They may work with cross-functional teams, including designers, developers, and business stakeholders, to create and bring new products to market.

These are just a few examples of the many roles and opportunities available within the tech industry. Whether you are interested in software development, data science, project management, cybersecurity, or another area of tech, a rewarding career path is waiting for you.

In addition to the roles listed above, many other positions within the tech industry may interest individuals without a technical background. For example, there are opportunities in marketing, sales, customer support, data, product and human resources, to name just a few. These roles may not require a deep technical understanding. Still, they require a strong understanding of the technology and the industry itself, as well as strong communication, analytical, and organisational skills.

One important thing to remember when transitioning into the tech industry is that it is a highly competitive field and may take some time and effort to gain the necessary skills and experience to be successful. This is particularly true for those from non-technical backgrounds looking to break into the field.

However, many resources are available to help individuals learn about the tech industry and gain the skills and experience needed to succeed. For example, online courses, boot camps, and certification programs can help individuals develop the soft skills needed for a tech career. Many networking opportunities, such as meetups and conferences, can help individuals connect with others in the industry and gain exposure to the latest technologies and trends.

In addition, many organisations and initiatives are dedicated to helping individuals from non-technical backgrounds transition into tech careers. For example, some organisations provide training, mentorship, and networking opportunities to individuals looking to break into the tech industry. Some programs offer paid internships and certification from accredited bodies for non-technical roles in tech. Job placement assistance and other support services to help individuals get started in their careers. An example will be the Prince 2 or PMP certification for project managers, CBAP for Business Analysis, etc.

It is also important to remember that the tech industry is constantly evolving and changing and that it is essential to stay up to date with the latest technologies and trends. This may require ongoing learning and professional development and a willingness to adapt and embrace new technologies as they emerge.

Despite the challenges, however, a career in the tech industry can be enriching personally and professionally. It is a field that offers a high degree of autonomy and creativity, as well as the opportunity to work on cutting-edge technologies and projects. And for those willing to put in the time and effort to gain the necessary skills and experience, it can be a lucrative and fulfilling career path.

Ultimately, for those interested in transitioning into a tech career without a technical background, the key to success is to be proactive and persistent and master critical soft skills. This may mean taking courses, getting certified, attending networking events, and seeking mentorship and support from others in the industry. But with hard work and dedication, it is possible to make a successful transition into a tech career and to make a positive impact on the world through technology.

Understanding the industry:

In addition to understanding the industry and gaining the necessary skills and experience, it is also essential to cultivate a strong network in the tech field. This can be done by attending industry events, participating in online forums and discussion groups, and connecting with others in the industry through social media platforms like LinkedIn. Building a network of contacts and connections within the tech industry can help individuals stay up-to-date on the latest trends and technologies and provide valuable support and guidance as they navigate their careers.

Another critical factor to consider when transitioning into a tech career is the type of company or organisation you want to work for. There are many different types of companies in the tech industry, including startups, established tech firms, and large Corporations. Each type of company has its unique culture, benefits, and opportunities, and it is essential to consider what is most important to you when deciding where to work.

Example:

For example, startups may offer a fast-paced, dynamic work environment and the opportunity to work on cutting-edge projects but may not provide the same stability and benefits as a larger, established company. On the other hand, established tech firms may offer more stability, benefits, and opportunities for advancement but may not offer a different level of creativity and autonomy than a startup.

Another essential factor to consider is the type of role you want to play within the tech industry. Some individuals may be interested in more hands-on roles, such as software development or data science, and product management. In contrast, others may be more interested in roles that are more focused on strategy and management, such as project management or business development.

Ultimately, the most important thing is, to be honest with yourself about your strengths, interests, and goals and to choose a career path that is aligned with your values and aspirations. With the proper training, experience, and support, it is possible to successfully transition into a tech career, regardless of your background or technical expertise.

Remember that a career in the tech industry is not a one-time decision but rather an ongoing journey of learning, growth, and evolution. As the industry continues to evolve and change, it is essential to be open to new opportunities, embrace new technologies and trends, and be willing to continuously adapt and develop your skills and knowledge.

Assessment

- How do the different types of businesses and organisations in the tech industry differ?

- What are some of the different roles available in the tech industry, and what are some of the critical skills required for each?

- What challenges do individuals interested in pursuing a career in the tech industry face, and how can they overcome them?

Chapter III

Learn the ins and outs of the tech industry from a non-technical perspective and overcome barriers to entry.

As a non-technical person, entering the tech industry can seem daunting. There are many soft skills and concepts to learn, as well as a culture that can sometimes feel intimidating and foreign. However, with the right approach and resources, anyone can overcome these barriers to entry and succeed in the tech industry.

Technical Skills:

This is a barrier but not a limitation. Also, because there are numerous non-technical roles, as long as you develop the soft skills you need and, most importantly, have the proper certifications to back up your skill, you can easily transition without any hurdles.

Industry Know-how:

Another barrier to entry for non-technical people in the tech industry is a need for more understanding of the industry and culture. To overcome this, it is important to research and gain a deeper understanding of the industry, including the different types of companies and organisations that make up the industry, the various roles and opportunities available, and the latest trends and technologies.

You need to cultivate a strong network of contacts within the tech industry. This can be done by attending industry events, participating in online forums and discussion groups, and connecting with others in the industry through social media platforms like LinkedIn. A strong network can provide valuable support, guidance, and opportunities for growth and advancement within the tech industry.

Growth Mindset:

You also need to have a growth mindset and be open to learning and change. The tech industry is constantly evolving and changing, and it is important to be willing to continuously adapt and develop your skills and knowledge to keep up.

How to overcome these barriers.

A critical aspect of overcoming barriers to entry in the tech industry as a non-technical person is developing a solid understanding of technology and its applications. This also includes understanding each stakeholder's different roles and responsibilities to communicate effectively with players in the space. Many resources are available for learning about these concepts, including online courses, tutorials, and books. If you purchased this book, you would have received a free short document on some of these concepts to aid your progress.

Additionally, you need to get mentors, internships, or freelance positions to gain experience. Experience is so critical to gain quick access to the industry or, better still, getting a certification that shows you have competence. Several companies offer programs that can help you gain experiences, such as the fully funded nano degrees by Udacity or the digital skills program by Google.

It's worth noting that you need to develop a strong understanding of the business side of the tech industry to be successful. You need a comprehensive understanding of how technology is used to solve business problems and how technology companies generate revenue and grow their businesses. This understanding can be achieved through various means, such as taking courses or workshops on business and entrepreneurship, reading relevant books and articles, or working in the field. You can check out Udemy or Coursera for online courses or go to amazon audible or books to get some books online.

In my experience, I would suggest you read The Lean Startup by Eric Ries, Crossing the Chasm by Geoffrey Moore, The Innovator's Dilemma by Clayton Christensen and my all-time favourite, Zero to One by Peter Thiel. This is a good starting point to gain some business knowledge that can help you in the tech industry.

For instance, courses or workshops on business and entrepreneurship can provide individuals with a strong foundation in business concepts, such as market analysis, product development, and financial management. These courses can also help individuals understand how technology companies use these concepts to create successful products and generate revenue.

Challenges faced by non-techie people

Lack of Confidence in your abilities is one of the challenges that non-technical people in the tech industry often face. This could be especially true when surrounded by highly technical colleagues.

The simple and quick fix for this is to focus on your strengths and skills, be confident about them and communicate with people effectively. Also, you may need to surround yourself with supportive and encouraging people and seek out mentors and coaches who can help you develop your skills and grow your confidence.

The ability to Network is another challenge faced by some non-technical individuals in the technical space. Networking allows you to build relationships, learn from others, and gain exposure to new opportunities and projects. Building strong relationships with others in the industry can help you find new opportunities, gain valuable insights and advice, and stay connected to the latest trends and developments.

To overcome this, you need to attend industry events, join online communities and discussion groups and connect with others in the tech industry on social media platforms like LinkedIn. Make sure to bring your unique skills, perspectives, and experiences to these interactions, and be open to learning and growing from others.

Another challenge is the ability to **Adapt to Change**. To succeed as a non-technical person in the tech industry, it is important to continuously learn and grow as the ecosystem changes at an unprecedented pace. You certainly need to keep up. You must stay up-to-date with the latest trends and technologies and continuously develop your skills and knowledge. This can be done through attending conferences and workshops, participating in online courses and tutorials, and reading relevant books and articles.

Another challenge non-technical people face is a lack of building a **Personal Brand**. Your brand is the perception that others have of you based on your skills, knowledge, and reputation. Building a strong personal brand can help you stand out and increase your visibility and credibility within the industry. Consider creating a professional website, participating in online forums and discussion groups, and sharing your thoughts and insights on relevant topics to gain acceptance and recognition in the industry.

Lastly, not properly **Understanding the Roles and Opportunities** in the industry could be a challenge. While many people associate the tech industry with software engineering and programming, many other roles and opportunities do not require core technical skills. For example, product managers and business analysts are critical to the success of tech companies, as they help companies reach new customers and generate revenue. Project management, human resources, and customer support roles are also important for the smooth operation of tech companies. A clear understanding of the different roles and opportunities within the industry will help you properly engage each stakeholder and collaborate effectively with cross-functional teams.

As advice, you need to develop a positive and growth-oriented mindset. The tech industry can be challenging sometimes, but it is also an exciting and rewarding workplace. Be open to new opportunities and experiences, and embrace the challenges that come your way. With the right approach, you can overcome the barriers to entry and succeed as a non-technical person in the tech industry.

Job options for non-technical people

Working in the product department is a good way to join the industry. Let's discuss a role in the product department, product management. Product managers are responsible for overseeing the development of new products and services, from idea to launch. They work closely with engineering and design teams to ensure that the product meets customers' needs, and they are also responsible for setting product strategy and driving growth.

To become a good product manager, you need to have strong communication skills, a deep understanding of the market and customer needs, and the ability to work well in a cross-functional team.

Another department to consider is Project, and a pivotal role to discuss is the Project management role. Project management plays a critical role in the success of any development project. A **Project Manager (PM)** oversees the planning, execution, and tracking of a specific short-term project. They ensure that the project is completed on time, within budget, and to the satisfaction of all stakeholders. The role of the Project Manager is crucial for the success of a development project as they play a key role in ensuring that the project is completed on time, within budget, and to the quality standards required. A PM must have excellent planning, organisational, and communication skills, as they are responsible for coordinating the efforts of the development team, stakeholders, and other parties involved in the project.

You can also consider the business department to work in business development. Business development professionals help tech companies grow by establishing partnerships, licensing agreements, and other strategic relationships with other companies. They are responsible for identifying new opportunities, negotiating deals, and building relationships with key stakeholders. In business development, you must have strong communication and negotiation skills, and a deep understanding of the tech industry and the competitive landscape.

In addition to these roles, there are many other roles and opportunities for non-technical people in the tech industry. These roles include customer support, quality assurance or tester, risk manager, and more.

Finding the right roles for you

You need to be able to identify and classify your strengths and interests. After you have done that, you need to marry that to different tech roles available. Once you have been able to identify the right role for you, then you need to focus on developing the skills and knowledge you need to succeed.

These include both understanding the usage of technical tools, such as data analysis and marketing tools, roadmapping and prototyping tools, wire-framing tools and soft skills, such as communication, problem solving and collaboration.

Consider taking courses and workshops, and participating in projects and internships to develop these skills and gain practical experience.

To be successful you need to be persistent and stay focused on your goals. The tech industry can be challenging and competitive, but with hard work and determination, you can overcome the barriers to entry and succeed.

Stay positive and focused, and don't be discouraged by setbacks or challenges. With the right approach, you can overcome the barriers to entry and enjoy a rewarding and fulfilling career in the tech industry.

As advice, you need to be mindful of work-life balance in the tech industry. The fast-paced and demanding nature of the industry can make it easy to get caught up in work, and neglect other important aspects of life such as family, friends, and personal interests. Take care of yourself and make time for the things that matter to you outside of work, to maintain your physical and mental health, and avoid burnout.

Assessment

- What are some of the common misconceptions about the tech industry, especially for those who are not from a technical background?

- What are some of the key concepts and terminology that non-technical individuals should be familiar with in order to better understand the tech industry?

- What are some of the strategies that non-technical individuals can use to overcome barriers to entry and pursue a career in the tech industry?

Chapter IV

The different non-technical roles in the tech industry

The tech industry offers a wide range of opportunities for non-technical people, beyond just software development or engineering. Understanding the different non-technical roles in the tech industry can help you identify the right path for you and achieve success in your career.

Project Management:

One of the most common non-technical roles in the tech industry is **project management**.

The role of a project manager in tech is critical in ensuring that projects are completed successfully within scope, budget, and schedule. They oversee the development and delivery of technology projects, ensuring that they are completed on time, within budget, and to the required quality standards. Project managers are responsible for planning, executing, and monitoring projects from start to finish. They work closely with stakeholders, team members, and resources to ensure that projects are completed efficiently and effectively.

The following are some of the key responsibilities of a project manager in tech:

1. Planning: Project managers are responsible for developing a project plan that outlines the project

scope, budget, timeline, and resources required to complete the project successfully. This involves working closely with stakeholders to understand their requirements and expectations.

2. Communication: Project managers are responsible for communicating project updates to stakeholders, team members, and resources throughout the project lifecycle. This involves setting expectations, providing progress reports, and managing any issues or risks that arise.

3. Risk management: Project managers are responsible for identifying and managing risks throughout the project lifecycle. This involves proactively identifying potential issues, developing contingency plans, and taking action to mitigate risks.

4. Budget management: Project managers are responsible for managing project budgets, ensuring that projects are completed within budget constraints.

5. Resource management: Project managers manage project resources, including people, technology, and materials. This involves ensuring that the right resources are available at the right time and managing resource allocation to ensure that projects are completed on time.

One example of successful project management in tech is the development of the iPhone. Apple's project management team was responsible for developing and implementing a plan to design, manufacture, and launch the iPhone. They worked closely with stakeholders, team members, and resources to ensure the project was completed within budget and on time. The project management team also identified and managed risks throughout the project lifecycle, ensuring that the launch of the iPhone was a success.

Another example is the development of the SpaceX Falcon Heavy rocket. Project managers at SpaceX were responsible for planning and executing the development of the rocket. They worked closely with stakeholders, team members, and resources to ensure the project was completed within budget and on time. The project management team also managed risks throughout the project lifecycle, ensuring the rocket's launch succeeded.

Successful project management in tech requires a combination of technical knowledge, communication skills, and leadership ability. They need strong organisational, communication, and leadership skills and a solid understanding of the software development process.

Product Management:

Another important non-technical role in the tech industry is **product management**.

Product management is a key function in developing and succeeding products and services a company offers. Product Managers are responsible for defining, developing, and bringing a product to market. They play a critical role in the overall strategy and direction by aligning product development efforts with its goals and objectives.

The responsibilities of a Product Manager include conducting market research, defining product requirements, developing product roadmaps, and working with cross-functional teams such as engineering, design, marketing, and sales to bring a product to market. PMs must also continuously monitor and analyze market trends, customer feedback, and competitive activities to ensure that their products remain relevant and competitive.

One of the key responsibilities of a Product manager is to understand the needs of the target customer and to develop a deep understanding of the market and competition. They use this knowledge to identify and prioritize product features, and to develop a product roadmap that outlines the development of the product over time. Product managers must also work closely with engineering and design teams to ensure that product requirements are clearly defined and that the product is being developed in a way that meets the target customer's needs.

Another responsibility of a product manager is to work with marketing, sales, and other cross-functional teams to develop and execute a successful go-to-market strategy. This may include defining the target market, developing pricing and positioning strategies, and creating product collateral such as brochures, datasheets, and website content. Product managers must also work closely with sales teams to ensure that the product is being sold effectively and that customer feedback is incorporated into the product development process.

In summary, Product managers are responsible for defining the product vision, developing the product roadmap, and working with cross-functional teams to ensure that products are developed and launched successfully. In tech, product managers play a critical role in bringing new products to market and improving existing products to meet customer needs.

The following are some of the key responsibilities of a product manager in tech:

1. Market research: Product managers are responsible for understanding the market and customers' needs. This involves researching customer needs, preferences, and pain points.

2. Product strategy: Product managers are responsible for developing a product strategy that aligns with business objectives and market needs. This involves defining the product vision, identifying target customers, and developing the product roadmap.

3. Product development: Product managers work closely with cross-functional teams, including designers, developers, and marketers, to develop and launch products. This involves overseeing product development from ideation to launch, including defining product features, prioritising features, and overseeing the development process.

4. Product marketing: Product managers are responsible for developing product marketing strategies that ensure products are launched successfully. This involves developing go-to-market plans, creating marketing collateral, and working with the marketing team to execute marketing campaigns.

5. Product analytics: Product managers track product

performance and make data-driven decisions. This involves monitoring product metrics, conducting A/B tests, and using data to improve the product.

One example of successful product management in tech is the development and launch of the Tesla Model S. Product managers at Tesla were responsible for developing the product strategy, overseeing product development, and ensuring the successful launch of the car. They worked closely with designers, engineers, and marketers to create a product that aligned with market needs and exceeded customer expectations. The product managers at Tesla also used data and customer feedback to make product improvements and ensure the product's ongoing success.

Another example is the development and launch of the Amazon Echo. Product managers at Amazon were responsible for developing the product strategy, overseeing product development, and ensuring the successful launch of the Echo. They worked closely with engineers, marketers, and user experience designers to create a product that was innovative, easy to use and met the market's needs. The product managers at Amazon also used data and customer feedback to make product improvements and ensure the product's ongoing success.

Successful product management in tech requires technical knowledge, business acumen, and leadership ability.

Business Analyst:

Another key role in the tech industry is **Business Analysis**.

The role of a business analyst in tech is to bridge the gap between business needs and technology solutions. Business analysts are responsible for analysing business requirements, identifying solutions, and ensuring that technology solutions meet business needs. In tech, business analysts play a critical role in defining requirements, developing functional specifications, and working with development teams to ensure that technology solutions are implemented successfully.

The following are some of the key responsibilities of a business analyst in tech:

1. Requirements analysis: Business analysts are responsible for identifying and documenting business requirements. This involves conducting stakeholder interviews, analysing business processes, and defining functional requirements.

2. Solution identification: Business analysts are responsible for identifying and recommending technology solutions that meet business needs. This involves researching technology options, evaluating potential solutions, and recommending the best solution.

3. Functional specification development: Business analysts are responsible for developing functional specifications that define how technology solutions will meet business needs. This involves creating user stories, use cases, and other documentation that describes how technology solutions will work.

4. Collaboration with development teams: Business

analysts work closely with development teams to ensure technology solutions are developed according to business requirements. This involves collaborating on the developing technical solutions, defining testing requirements, and facilitating communication between business stakeholders and development teams.

5. Business process improvement: Business analysts are responsible for identifying opportunities for business process improvement. This involves analysing business processes and recommending changes to improve efficiency, reduce costs, and enhance the customer experience.

One example of successful business analysis in tech is the development and launch of the Starbucks mobile app. Business analysts at Starbucks were responsible for identifying business requirements, recommending technology solutions, and working with development teams to ensure that the app met business needs. They conducted stakeholder interviews, analysed business processes, and defined functional requirements to ensure the app would enhance the customer experience. The business analysts at Starbucks also collaborated closely with development teams to ensure that the app was developed according to business requirements.

Another example is the implementation of a new HR system at an HR tech startup, KlevaHR. Business analysts were responsible for analyzing business requirements, identifying technology solutions, and developing functional specifications for the new system. They worked closely with HR stakeholders to ensure that the new system met business needs and complied with regulatory requirements. The business analysts also collaborated with development teams to ensure that the new system was developed and implemented successfully.

The role of a business analyst is critical to the success of technology solutions. Business analysts are responsible for analyzing business requirements, identifying solutions, and ensuring that technology solutions meet business needs.

Successful business analysis in tech requires a combination of technical knowledge, business acumen, and communication skills.

Design:

Design is another important non-technical area in the tech industry.

Designers are responsible for creating the look and feel of technology products, from user interfaces and websites to mobile apps and software. Designers need a strong understanding of design principles, user-centred design, and a keen eye for detail. User Experience (UX) designers are responsible for creating intuitive and user-friendly products, websites, and applications. They work to ensure that the overall user experience is positive, seamless, and meets the target user's needs. UX designers use various tools and techniques to understand the needs of the target user and design user-centred products. This may include user research, creating personas and scenarios, and conducting usability testing.

One of the key tools UX designers use is wireframing and prototyping software. Wireframes are simple, black-and-white diagrams that outline the structure and content of a website or application. Prototyping tools allow UX designers to create interactive prototypes that simulate a product's look, feel, and functionality, allowing users to interact with the product and provide feedback. Examples of wireframing and prototyping tools include Sketch, Figma, Adobe XD, and InVision.

In general, a designer's role in tech is to create and optimise digital products and experiences, such as websites, mobile applications, and user interfaces. Designers play a critical role in developing technology solutions by ensuring they are both functional and aesthetically pleasing.

In tech, design is not just about making things look good but also about ensuring they are usable, accessible, and engaging for users.

The following are some of the key responsibilities of a designer in tech:

1. User research: Designers are responsible for understanding the needs and preferences of the target audience. This involves conducting user research, such as user interviews, surveys, and usability testing, to gain insights into user behaviour and preferences.
2. User interface design: Designers are responsible for creating the visual design of technology solutions, such as the layout, color scheme, typography, and iconography. They ensure that the design is consistent

with the brand identity and is visually appealing.

3. User experience design: Designers are responsible for creating the overall user experience of technology solutions. This involves designing user flows, wireframes, and prototypes to ensure that the technology solution is easy to use, accessible, and engaging for users.

4. Collaboration with development teams: Designers work closely with development teams to ensure that the technology solution is implemented according to design specifications. They provide guidance on design elements, such as layout, typography, and color scheme, and work with developers to ensure that the design is implemented correctly.

5. Design optimisation: Designers are responsible for continuously optimising the design of technology solutions. This involves analysing user feedback and data, such as user behaviour, to identify areas for improvement and make design changes accordingly.

One example of successful design in tech is redesigning the Airbnb website. Designers at Airbnb were responsible for conducting user research, creating wireframes, and designing the website's overall user interface and user experience. They analysed user feedback and data to identify areas for improvement, such as the booking process and made design changes accordingly. The redesign resulted in a significant increase in bookings and user engagement.

Another example is the redesign of the Slack messaging app. Designers at Slack were responsible for creating a new design that improved the user experience and streamlined the messaging process. They worked closely with development teams to ensure that the new design was implemented according to specifications. The redesign resulted in increased user engagement and a more efficient messaging experience.

Successful design in tech requires a combination of user research, design skills, and collaboration with development teams.

Human Resources:

Human resources is another critical area responsible for attracting, developing, hiring, and retaining the best talent in the fast-paced and competitive technology industry. Human resources professionals need a deep understanding of the tech industry, the skills and knowledge required for different roles, and the trends and challenges facing the industry.

HR professionals work closely with hiring managers, executives, and employees to ensure that the company's workforce is aligned with its goals and values, and they also provide support and resources to employees to help them succeed in their roles.

The following are some of the key responsibilities of HR professionals in tech:

1. Recruitment and Talent Acquisition: HR professionals in tech are responsible for finding and recruiting top talent to fill various technical and non-technical roles within the company. They work closely with hiring

managers to identify and assess candidates, negotiate offers, and coordinate onboarding processes.

2. Employee Relations: HR professionals are responsible for creating and maintaining a positive work environment for employees, including handling employee complaints, providing resources for employee well-being, and ensuring compliance with workplace laws and regulations.

3. Performance Management: HR professionals work with managers to set and track performance goals, provide feedback to employees, and provide support and guidance for employees to succeed in their roles.

4. Learning and Development: HR professionals in tech are responsible for providing resources and training to employees to help them develop new skills, keep up with industry trends and best practices, and grow within their roles.

5. Diversity and Inclusion: HR professionals play a key role in promoting diversity and inclusion within the tech industry by creating initiatives to attract and retain underrepresented groups, fostering a culture of inclusivity, and developing policies to support diversity and equity.

One example of successful HR in tech is the diversity and inclusion initiative implemented by Pinterest. The company's HR team recognized the need for greater diversity and inclusion in the technology industry and created an initiative to attract and retain underrepresented groups, including women and people of color. As part of the initiative, Pinterest provided resources and training for employees on diversity and inclusion, developed partnerships with diverse organizations, and set ambitious diversity targets. As a result of the initiative, Pinterest has increased the number of underrepresented groups within its workforce, and its efforts have been recognized as a model for diversity and inclusion in the tech industry.

Another example is the recruitment and talent acquisition strategy implemented by Google's HR team. Google is known for its rigorous hiring processes and HR professionals are responsible for identifying and attracting top talent to fill various technical and non-technical roles within the company. Google's HR team leverages data and analytics to identify the best candidates and employs a range of recruiting tactics, such as offering competitive compensation and benefits packages, providing training and development opportunities, and creating a positive company culture. As a result of its recruitment and talent acquisition strategy, Google has become one of the most successful technology companies in the world.

HR professionals are responsible for attracting, developing, and retaining top talent, promoting a positive work environment, and fostering diversity and inclusion within the industry.

Successful HR in tech requires a combination of recruitment and talent acquisition strategies, performance management, learning and development initiatives, and a commitment to diversity and inclusion.

Customer support:

Customer support is an essential role in the tech industry. Customer support professionals are responsible for helping customers with their technology-related questions and issues and providing high-quality customer service. Customer support professionals need strong communication and interpersonal skills, as well as a solid understanding of the technology and its applications.

The primary responsibility of customer support is to assist customers in using and troubleshooting products or services provided by the company. They play a vital role in ensuring that customers have a positive experience and remain loyal to the company. In addition, customer support provides valuable feedback to the product development team, which can help improve products and services.

The following are some of the key responsibilities of customer support in tech:

1. Product Support: Customer support representatives provide technical support to customers using the company's products or services. They may assist with product installation, provide troubleshooting support, or answer customer questions about the product's features and capabilities.
2. Customer Service: Customer support representatives are responsible for providing high-quality customer service to customers. They may respond to customer inquiries or complaints, provide billing support, or offer guidance on using the company's products or services effectively.

3. Feedback Collection: Customer support representatives collect valuable feedback from customers that can help improve products and services. They may report bugs, suggest product enhancements, or provide insights into customer behavior and preferences.

4. Continuous Improvement: Customer support representatives play an essential role in the continuous improvement of products and services. They provide insights and feedback to the product development team, which can help improve product design, features, and overall customer experience.

One example of successful customer support in tech is Zappos, an online shoe retailer that has become known for its exceptional customer service. Zappos is committed to providing the best possible customer experience, and its customer support representatives are empowered to go above and beyond to ensure customer satisfaction. Zappos provides extensive training to its customer support team and encourages representatives to develop personal connections with customers, which has helped to build a loyal customer base.

Another example is the customer support provided by Apple. Apple is known for its customer-centric approach and has developed a robust support system to assist customers with its products and services. Apple offers various support channels, including phone, email, and online chat support, and has developed an extensive knowledge base to help customers troubleshoot common issues. In addition, Apple provides in-person support at its retail stores, where customers can receive one-on-one assistance from a Genius Bar specialist.

In summary, customer support plays a crucial role in the tech industry by providing technical support, offering customer service, collecting feedback, and supporting continuous improvement.

Successful customer support requires a commitment to high-quality service, ongoing training and development, and a willingness to go above and beyond to ensure customer satisfaction. Companies that prioritize customer support, such as Zappos and Apple, have become known for their exceptional customer service and have developed loyal customer bases as a result.

All these non-technical roles in the tech industry play a crucial role in the success of technology companies and organizations. Whether it's project management, product management, design, human resources, or customer support, each role brings a unique set of skills and knowledge that is essential for the smooth operation and growth of the company.

Non-technical roles are not limited to only the ones discussed above, there are a number of other roles such as marketing and sales, data analyst, data analysis, quality assurance or tester, business development and so many other roles.

Assessment

- A fill-in-the-blank exercise where the reader has to identify different non-technical roles available in the tech industry, and what are some of the key responsibilities and tasks associated with each?

● How do non-technical roles in the tech industry differ from non-technical roles in other industries?

● What are some of the key skills that are required for success in non-technical roles in the tech industry?

Chapter V

Analyze how your existing skills can be applied to a non-technical tech job

To make a successful transition to a non-technical tech career, it's important to analyze your existing skills and determine how they can be applied to a role in the tech industry. This will help you identify your strengths and potential areas for growth, and can also help you make informed decisions about which roles and companies to pursue.

Skills Inventory:

One place to start is by conducting a skills inventory. This involves making a list of all of your existing skills, both technical and non-technical, and evaluating how they might be relevant to a non-technical tech job. For example, if you have strong communication skills, you might consider roles such as project management, marketing or customer support. If you have project management experience, you might consider business analysis, product management or program management roles.

Experience and Background:

Another factor to consider is your experience and background. Think about the types of industries or organizations you have worked in, and how these experiences might be relevant to the tech industry. For example, if you have experience working in finance, you might consider roles such as financial analyst or business operations. If you have experience in retail, you might consider roles such as tester, product manager or e-commerce specialist.

Interest and Passion:

It's also important to consider your interests and passions, as these can be valuable assets in the tech industry. For example, if you are passionate about sustainability, you might consider roles related to clean energy or sustainable technology. If you have a passion for gaming, you might consider roles related to game design or user experience.

Feedback:

In addition to conducting a skills inventory and considering your experience and passions, it can also be helpful to seek feedback from others, such as friends, family, or colleagues. They may have valuable insights into your strengths and skills that you may not have considered, and can also provide you with guidance and advice as you navigate the tech industry.

Soft Skills:

Soft skills are essential in the tech industry, where collaboration, communication, and creativity are critical for success. The following are some of the key soft skills required in tech:

Soft Skill	Description	Importance
Communication	The ability to clearly and effectively convey information to others	Crucial for collaboration, teamwork, and project management
Creativity	The ability to think outside the box and develop innovative solutions to problems	Critical for product development, design, and marketing
Critical Thinking	The ability to analyze and evaluate information to make informed decisions	Essential for problem-solving, decision-making, and strategy development
Adaptability	The ability to be flexible and adjust to changing circumstances or requirements	Critical for working in a fast-paced and constantly changing industry
Empathy	The ability to understand and connect with others on an emotional level	Crucial for customer support, user experience, and team dynamics
Leadership	The ability to inspire and guide others towards a common goal	Essential for project management, team leadership, and organizational strategy
Time Management	The ability to effectively manage time and prioritize	Crucial for meeting deadlines, completing projects, and

tasks   maintaining productivity

One example of a tech company that values soft skills is Google. Google's hiring process is designed to identify candidates with strong soft skills, including communication, problem-solving, and leadership. Google's approach is to hire for "learning ability" rather than specific technical skills, as they believe that soft skills are essential for success in the tech industry.

Another example is Airbnb, a company that values creativity and innovation. Airbnb's culture emphasizes creativity and experimentation, and they encourage their employees to take risks and explore new ideas. This culture has led to numerous successful product launches, such as the "Experiences" feature, which allows travelers to book unique activities and experiences with local hosts.

Companies that value soft skills, such as Google and Airbnb, have been able to attract and retain top talent and drive innovation in the industry. The key soft skills required in tech include communication, creativity, critical thinking, adaptability, empathy, leadership, and time management, and individuals with these skills are highly valued in the industry.

It's important to note that there are additional soft skills which would be critical based on the role you have selected in addition to the above general top soft skills. It's important to find out those specific skills as it relates to your desired role.

Example:

For example, if you have strong communication skills, you might consider roles such as product marketing, marketing, or business development, where you can use your communication skills to build relationships with customers and partners or to create compelling marketing campaigns. If you have strong problem-solving skills, you might consider roles such as product management, where you can use your skills to analyze customer needs and identify solutions to meet those needs.

You need to consider your ability to learn and adapt, as the tech industry is constantly evolving and changing. If you have a strong desire to learn and grow and are comfortable with uncertainty and change, you may be well suited for roles in the tech industry.

Bringing it all together

When applying for non-technical tech jobs, it's important to highlight your existing skills and experiences in your resume and cover letter and to tailor your application to the specific role and company you are applying to. This can include emphasizing your relevant experiences, interest, passion, skills, and achievements, and demonstrating how you would be an asset to the company.

You should research companies and organizations in the tech industry to identify those that align with your values, interests, and career goals. This can help you find a company and role that is a good fit for you and can increase your chances of success and satisfaction in your non-technical tech career.

By taking the time to analyze your existing skills and background, and by seeking feedback and pursuing continuous learning and development opportunities, you can better understand how your skills can be applied to a non-technical tech job, and make a successful transition to a career in the tech industry.

To continuously learn and acquire new skills is to seek out training and development opportunities, such as online courses, boot camps, and workshops. This can help you stay current with new technologies and trends, and can also help you develop new skills and knowledge that are relevant to your non-technical tech career.

To succeed, you should be willing to take risks, and to step outside of your comfort zone. This can include taking on new projects, exploring new areas of the tech industry, and seeking out new job opportunities that align with your skills and interests.

It's also crucial to understand the importance of communication skills in the tech industry, as non-technical roles often require collaboration with technical teams and stakeholders. Good communication skills can help you build strong relationships and effectively communicate complex ideas to individuals with different backgrounds and expertise levels.

To enhance your communication skills, you can practice active listening, asking questions and seeking feedback. Additionally, you can work on your writing and presentation skills by writing clear and concise emails, creating compelling presentations, and delivering engaging talks.

The ability to think critically and solve problems must be properly utilized. Many non-technical tech roles involve problem-solving and decision-making, and it's essential to have strong critical thinking skills to be successful in these roles.

To improve your critical thinking skills, you can practice analyzing complex problems and developing creative solutions. You can also seek out opportunities to collaborate with individuals from diverse backgrounds, as this can help you broaden your perspective and develop new ideas and approaches.

A strong project management skills is important in a number of roles. Many non-technical tech roles involve managing projects and ensuring that they are delivered on time, within budget, and to a high standard of quality.

To develop your project management skills, you can seek out training and development opportunities, such as online courses, workshops, and certification programs. You can also practice using project management tools and techniques, such as agile project management and scrum, to better manage projects and ensure that projects are delivered successfully.

It's important to have a strong understanding of the business side of the tech industry, as many non-technical tech roles involve business development, marketing, and sales. Understanding the financial, legal, and regulatory aspects of the tech industry can help you make informed decisions and effectively negotiate deals and contracts.

To develop your business skills, you can seek out training and development opportunities, such as online courses, workshops, and business school programs. You can also seek out mentorship and coaching opportunities, as these can help you gain insight and advice from experienced individuals in the tech industry.

Assessment

• What are some of the key skills and strengths that you possess that might be relevant to non-technical roles in the tech industry?

• How might you go about identifying which non-technical roles in the tech industry are the best match for your skills and interests?

• What are some of the strategies that you can use to develop or enhance the skills that are most important for success in non-technical roles in the tech industry?

Chapter VI

Apply your relevant skills to real-world scenarios related to non-technical tech jobs

Applying your relevant skills to real-world scenarios related to non-technical tech jobs is an essential step in successfully transitioning to a tech career. To do this, it's important first to identify your existing skills and experience, and then determine how these can be applied to various non-technical tech roles.

Success Stories

As a technical consultant, I had the privilege to work with some amazing individuals who were passionate about transitioning to the tech industry. One such person was Danny, who was the Head of Marketing Communications at a top FMCG company in Africa.

Although he longed to work in the tech industry, there were no opportunities available at his office. During our one-on-one coaching session, we were able to identify Danny's unique strengths, which included his ability to tell compelling stories, solve complex problems, empathize with others, listen actively, and write engaging content.

Together, we explored various career paths, and Danny decided to pursue a Business Analysis role. With our guidance, he enrolled in a program and completed the ECBA exam within two months, passing with flying colors.

A month later, Danny moved to the UK and secured a position at a top Consulting firm. His exceptional performance led to multiple job offers within six months, and he turned to us for guidance on how to proceed. By applying the principles outlined in this book in addition to our coaching program, Danny was able to achieve his career goals at an accelerated pace, a testament to his dedication and hard work.

Another inspiring individual I had the pleasure of working with was Tope, a customer care representative at a tech company in the UK. She had a burning desire to grow professionally, earn more, and become an industry expert in the field of technology.

Through our group coaching program, we introduced Tope to the principles outlined in this book, and she applied them with determination and focus. She decided to enroll in a Scrum training program, which she completed successfully within a month. Encouraged by her newfound skills, Tope applied for an open role in the project department at her company and was thrilled to secure the position. Her outstanding performance resulted in several offers from other companies, and she is now earning more than double her previous salary.

Tope's dedication to her professional development has been impressive, and she is currently preparing to sit for her Project Management Professional (PMP) exam to gain even more valuable skills for her next career move.

These examples demonstrate the transformative power of investing in oneself and applying the principles outlined in our books and programs. By identifying their unique strengths, setting clear goals, and taking concrete steps towards their objectives, Danny and Tope were able to achieve remarkable success in their chosen tech careers.

Non-technical professionals can leverage their relevant soft and business skills to excel in a range of non-technical tech jobs. The key is to identify the skills that you have and how they can be applied in a tech context. Some tips for applying your relevant soft and business skills to real-world scenarios in non-technical tech jobs

1. **Problem-Solving**: The tech industry is built on innovation and problem-solving. Non-technical professionals who are good at identifying problems and finding creative solutions can excel in tech jobs that require critical thinking and a strong problem-solving mindset. For instance, non-technical individuals can apply their problem-solving skills to areas like product development, customer support, and project management.

2. **Business Acumen**: The tech industry is not just about technology; it is also about business. Understanding the market, identifying opportunities, and creating business strategies are critical skills for success in tech. Non-technical professionals with experience in marketing, sales, finance, or operations can leverage their business acumen to excel in tech jobs that require

them to understand the commercial side of the tech industry.

3. **Adaptability**: The tech industry is fast-paced and ever-changing. Non-technical professionals who are adaptable and open to learning new skills and technologies can thrive in tech roles that require flexibility and the ability to pivot quickly. For example, non-technical individuals can leverage their adaptability in roles like project management, where they may be required to work on multiple projects with changing priorities and requirements.

4. **Creativity**: The tech industry is all about creating new solutions to old problems. Non-technical professionals who are creative and can think outside the box can excel in tech roles that require innovation and fresh ideas. For instance, non-technical individuals can apply their creativity to areas like content creation, design, and marketing.

Anyone can apply the principles discussed in this book and you can achieve your goal of working in tech seamlessly. In addition to the principles discussed so far, after completing your skill inventory process, applying your skills to real life scenarios would require you to consider the following and apply them correctly in order to succeed.

Gain relevant experience:

To be successful in a non-technical tech role, it's also important to have a strong understanding of the industry and the specific company or organization you're working for. This means researching and staying up-to-date on industry trends, as well as understanding the company's mission, values, and products or services.

You also need a strong work ethic and be a problem solver. Tech companies value individuals who can take ownership of their work and proactively find solutions to challenges that arise. Most importantly, opt-in for internship or freelance roles in order to gain the base experience in your chosen role.

Growth mindset and Soft skills:

To have a growth mindset and continuously seek to improve and develop your skills and knowledge is a must in the tech industry. The ecosystem is constantly evolving, and it's important to stay ahead of the curve and be open to learning new technologies and methods. This can be done through taking online courses or attending workshops and training sessions or taking certifications.

You need to build your soft skills such as the ability to effectively communicate with both technical and non-technical stakeholders or ability to translate technical concepts and ideas into plain language for those who may not have a technical background. Good communication skills also help you build strong relationships with colleagues and clients, and can lead to better collaboration and problem-solving.

Learn to understand the different types of technology and how they are used in various industries. For example, understanding the differences between cloud computing, software development, and data analytics can help you better understand the needs and requirements of a specific company or organization.

Get hands-on experience by working on projects or participating in activities such as hackathons. These events provide an opportunity to work with other professionals and learn about new technologies and methodologies, while also allowing you to showcase your skills and knowledge.

Networking:

Networking is another key aspect of transitioning to a tech career as a non-technical person. Building relationships with people in the tech industry can help you learn about new job opportunities, get advice and mentorship, and make important connections that can benefit you in your career.

Attending industry events, such as conferences and meetups, is a great way to network with professionals in the tech industry. These events allow you to meet and talk with people working in tech, learn about their experiences, and make valuable connections.

Online communities and professional networks, such as LinkedIn, can also be valuable resources for networking and learning about the tech industry. Joining groups related to tech or specific industries can help you connect with professionals, participate in discussions, and stay up-to-date on industry news and trends.

Personal Brand:

Having a strong online presence can also help you build your personal brand. This includes creating a professional and up-to-date

LinkedIn profile, having an active presence on social media, and maintaining a portfolio of your work and projects.

When applying for non-technical tech jobs, it's important to understand the specific requirements and responsibilities of the role. Researching the company and the role, as well as preparing for interviews and creating a strong resume and cover letter, can help increase your chances of landing the job.

It's also important to be flexible and open to new opportunities. The tech industry is rapidly changing and evolving, and being willing to adapt and learn new technologies and methodologies can help you stay ahead of the curve and be successful in your career.

Mentor:

Another good step for transitioning to a tech career as a non-technical person is to find a mentor. Having someone with experience in the tech industry to guide and support you can be invaluable. Mentors can provide you with advice, help you navigate the industry, and connect you with opportunities that align with your career goals.

Education:

Continuing education is also crucial in the tech industry. As technology evolves, it's important to keep your skills and knowledge up-to-date. This can include attending workshops, taking online courses, or even pursuing a higher degree in a related field. You can sign up for our coaching programs to gain the required education to take on certifications or to gain understanding of some of the roles and strategies discussed so far.

Having the right training or certification will help you build your confidence which would result in a passion for what you do and help build a good attitude to work. Having a strong work ethic and a positive attitude can also help you succeed in the tech industry. Employers value employees who are motivated, have strong attention to detail, and can work well in a team.

Culture and High Pay:

Another factor in transitioning to a tech career is understanding the culture of the tech industry. Tech companies and organizations often have a unique culture that values innovation, creativity, and collaboration. Understanding this culture and how it affects the workplace can help you feel more comfortable and succeed in your role.

When looking for non-technical tech jobs, it's also important to understand the different types of companies and organizations that make up the tech industry. This includes tech startups, established tech companies, and organizations that use technology to support their operations. Each type of organization may have different cultures, work environments, and opportunities for career growth.

An advantage of transitioning to a tech career is the potential to earn higher. Many non-technical tech jobs offer competitive salaries and benefits, such as project managers, product managers, and marketing specialists. However, it's important to keep in mind that salary and earning potential will vary depending on the organization and location. You can take on remote jobs and earn even more if you are able to work with cross functional teams made up of people with different cultures, backgrounds, locations and even roles.

Long term goal:

When transitioning to a tech career, you must understand your long-term goals. This can help you identify the right opportunities and make informed decisions about your career path. Whether you're interested in advancing in a specific role, starting your own tech company, or exploring other career paths, clearly understanding your goals can help guide your decisions and ensure your success in the tech industry.

You need to have a strong sense of purpose and direction. Knowing why you're pursuing a career in tech and what you hope to achieve can help you stay motivated and focused, even when faced with challenges and obstacles.

Competitive, Dynamic and Global:

Overall, you need to understand that the tech industry is highly competitive and dynamic. To succeed in a non-technical tech role, individuals must be able to adapt to change and be open to new challenges. You must also be able to work well in a fast-paced, highly collaborative environment. The tech industry values individuals who can work effectively in teams and can bring positive and productive energy to the workplace.

The tech industry is highly global. Many tech companies and organizations operate globally and offer opportunities for individuals to work in a variety of locations and with people from diverse backgrounds. Therefore, non-technical individuals who are highly adaptable and have strong cross-cultural skills can excel in roles such as project management, product management, business development, marketing, and even customer support. In these roles, they are responsible for building relationships with customers and partners from around the world and ensuring that their needs are met.

Remember, the tech industry is not just for those with a technical background, and there are many opportunities available for non-technical individuals with diverse skills and experience. So, don't let a lack of technical skills hold you back from pursuing a career in tech. You can make the transition and succeed in the industry with dedication and hard work.

Assessment

- What are some of the different types of projects or initiatives that non-technical individuals might work on in the tech industry?

- What are some of the common challenges that individuals in non-technical roles in the tech industry might face, and how can they be addressed?

- How can you demonstrate to potential employers that you have the skills and experience necessary to succeed in a non-technical role in the tech industry?

Chapter VII

Find out which career path best suits your interests and transferable skills by looking at the career advancement opportunities available in non-technical tech jobs

One of the key aspects of transitioning to a tech career as a non-technical person is evaluating the career progression opportunities available. This involves taking a closer look at the different non-technical roles in the tech industry and identifying which paths align with your transferable skills and interests.

Transferable Skills:

There are several non-technical roles in the tech industry, including product management, project management, design, sales, marketing, and customer support. Each of these roles has its own set of responsibilities and skills, and it is important to understand what each role entails before choosing the right path for you.

For example, if you are interested in the design aspect of tech, you may want to consider roles such as UX/UI designer or product designer. If you have a background in sales or marketing, then a role in product marketing or business development for a tech company may be a good fit.

On the other hand, if you have experience in customer service or support, then a role in customer support or technical support for a tech company may be a good fit.

Once you have identified the non-technical tech role that aligns with your transferable skills and interests, the next step is to evaluate the career progression opportunities within that role. Most non-technical tech roles have a clear path for progression, with the opportunity to advance from entry-level positions to more senior roles over time.

For example, in product management, you may start as a product coordinator and then progress to a product manager, then a senior product manager, and eventually a director of product management. In design, you may start as a junior designer and then progress to a senior designer and eventually a design lead or director.

One of the best ways to evaluate career progression opportunities is to research the roles and responsibilities of the positions you are interested in. You can look at job postings, talk to people in the industry, and attend networking events to gain a better understanding of the skills and experiences required for the role. This will give you a clear picture of the career paths available within your desired field and help you determine which aligns with your transferable skills and interests. As a guide, follow these processes below to understand how to decide properly on the career path.

Role and company consideration

When evaluating career progression opportunities, it is important to consider the role itself and the company you work for. Some tech companies are more established and may have more opportunities for career progression, while others are startups and may be more focused on growing their product or service.

You also need to consider the demand for the role within the tech industry. Certain non-technical tech positions, such as user experience (UX) designers and digital marketing managers, are in high demand due to the increasing importance placed on user-centered design and digital marketing efforts. By choosing a role that is in high demand, you increase your chances of finding job security and steady career progression.

In addition to considering the role, you must also look at the company culture, work environment, and compensation. These factors will play a role in your overall job satisfaction and can impact your ability to advance in your career.

Skills and Knowledge

When evaluating career progression opportunities, it's essential to consider the skills and knowledge required for each position. You need to be proactive in developing the skills necessary for advancement. For example, suppose you are interested in transitioning from a customer support role to a product management role. In that case, you should be proactive in learning about product development, market research, and product strategy. One way to do this is to take online courses or attend workshops and conferences related to product management. You can also network with other product managers and learn from their experiences and insights. Reading books, blogs, and articles about product management can also be a valuable source of information and inspiration.

You also need to consider the level of education and training required for each role. Some non-technical tech positions, such as project management or business analysis, may require a bachelor's degree or certification in a related field. However, many non-technical tech roles, such as customer success management or marketing, can be entered with only a high school diploma and relevant work experience.

For example, if you have strong interpersonal and communication skills, you may excel in a customer success management role. However, if you're more analytical and data-driven, a role in data analysis may be a better fit. By aligning your skills and interests with the requirements of a specific role, you increase your chances of success and satisfaction in your new career.

Seek Opportunity for growth in your current role

Another way to develop the skills necessary for career progression is to seek out opportunities for growth within your current role. For example, if you are a customer support specialist, you may want to volunteer to lead a project or take on additional responsibilities within the support team. This will not only help you develop new skills, but it will also demonstrate your ability and commitment to your current employer.

Career progression in the tech industry is wider than a single path. With the flexibility to move between roles and the potential to explore new areas of interest, you have the opportunity to build a diverse and fulfilling career in the tech industry. This versatility is one of the biggest draws of the tech industry for non-techies.

Industry trends and development

When evaluating career progression opportunities, it is also important to consider industry trends and developments. For example, the rise of artificial intelligence (AI) and machine learning (ML) is having a significant impact on many tech roles, including non-technical roles. As such, it is important to be knowledgeable about AI and ML and understand how they may impact your role in the future. Another example is the rise of automation, and artificial intelligence (AI) is leading to a demand for professionals with data analysis and machine learning skills. By understanding the industry landscape and the changes, you can position yourself for success by developing the skills and knowledge required for high-demand roles.

Impact of Tech on various industries

Additionally, you need to understand the impact of technology on multiple industries, as the tech industry is becoming increasingly intertwined with many other sectors. For example, the rise of e-commerce has significantly impacted the retail industry. Understanding this impact can be valuable for those pursuing careers in the tech industry.

High Compensation

Non-technical tech roles can be highly compensated, with salaries often being higher than those in traditional industries.

However, it is important to understand that compensation can vary widely based on the role, company, and location. It is noteworthy to consider other benefits, such as health insurance, paid time off, and retirement benefits, when evaluating a job offer.

Company culture

You need to consider the culture of the company you're interested in. Some tech companies may have a more relaxed, startup-like culture, while others may have a more traditional corporate atmosphere. Choosing a company whose values align with your own and where you feel comfortable and supported is important.

Lastly, talk to people in your network who work in the tech industry. This could include friends, family members, or even colleagues from your current job. They can give you an insider's perspective on the different roles and opportunities available within the industry and help you make a more informed decision about your career path.

Build your Portfolio

Building a portfolio can be an excellent way for non-technical individuals to showcase their business and soft skills and demonstrate their potential value to the tech industry. Here are some steps to help build a portfolio:

1. Identify your skills: The first step is to identify your business and soft skills that are relevant to the tech industry. These could be skills such as project management, communication, teamwork, problem-

solving, creativity, and critical thinking. Once you have identified your skills, think about how you can provide evidence of your expertise in these areas.

2. Choose projects to highlight: Identify the projects you have worked on that best demonstrate your skills. If you don't have any relevant projects, consider creating your own projects. Choose projects that are both challenging and relevant to the tech industry.

3. Create a summary of each project: Create a summary that includes the problem you were trying to solve, the actions you took to address the problem, and the results you achieved. Be sure to focus on the skills you used and how they contributed to the project's success.

4. Provide evidence of your skills: In addition to project summaries, you can provide additional evidence of your skills. This could include testimonials from colleagues or managers, reports, presentations, or other artifacts demonstrating your skills.

5. Organize your portfolio: Organize your portfolio clearly and concisely that highlights your skills and projects. You can use an online platform such as LinkedIn, GitHub, or a personal website to showcase your portfolio.

6. Share your portfolio: Once you have created it, be sure to share it with industry stakeholders such as recruiters, hiring managers, and potential colleagues. You can also include your portfolio in your job application materials and use it during interviews to help communicate your skills and experience.

As a use case, let's take John, a marketing professional interested in transitioning to the tech industry. He identifies his project management, communication, and problem-solving skills as relevant to the tech industry. John creates a portfolio with several projects he has worked on, including a successful product launch, a customer engagement campaign, and a cross-functional team project.

John provides a summary for each project highlighting his skills and contributions. He also includes testimonials from colleagues and reports he authored. John creates a LinkedIn profile and adds his portfolio to his profile. He shares his portfolio with recruiters and hiring managers in the tech industry and includes it in his job applications. Thanks to his portfolio, John can successfully transition to a non-technical role in the tech industry.

Assessment

A career planning exercise where the reader has to identify their transferable skills, interests, and career goals and then match them with appropriate non-technical tech jobs.

Chapter VIII

How to make a successful tech career transition

Making a successful transition from a non-technical career to a tech career can be challenging. Still, with the right preparation and mindset, it is possible. To make the most of your transition, it is important to understand the tech industry, its various opportunities, and how to make the most of your existing skills. Here are some key steps to making a successful tech career transition:

- **Conduct thorough research:** Before making any career move, it is vital to research the tech industry thoroughly and understand what it entails. This means learning about the various types of companies and organizations that make up the industry, the different roles and opportunities, and the skills and qualifications required for other positions.

- **Identify your transferable skills:** Before making a tech career transition, it is important to evaluate your existing skills and see how they can be applied to a non-technical tech job. This includes looking at areas such as project management, product management, customer support, business analyst, and more. Conduct a skill inventory to ascertain your skills and see how it fits into the role you are passionate about.

• **Network with professionals in the industry:** Networking is a critical aspect of any career transition, and the tech industry is no exception. This can involve reaching out to people who work in the industry and asking for advice, attending networking events and conferences, and connecting with industry groups on social media.

• **Get additional training and education:** Depending on the role you are interested in, you may need additional training or certification to be competitive in the tech industry. This can involve taking courses and certifications in areas such as product development, business analysis, data analysis, and others.

• **Build a portfolio:** A portfolio is a great way to showcase your skills and demonstrate your ability to work in a tech-related role. This can include examples of projects you have worked on, case studies, and testimonials from colleagues and clients.

• **Be flexible:** The tech industry is constantly evolving, and it is important to be flexible and adaptable to succeed. This means being willing to learn new skills, embrace new technologies, and take on new challenges.

• **Have a growth mindset:** Making a successful tech career transition requires a growth mindset, where you always look for ways to learn and improve. This means staying current with industry trends and developments, seeking new opportunities, and never being afraid to take risks.

Making a successful transition into the tech industry requires careful planning and execution. The first step is understanding what you want to achieve and how you plan to get there. Before making any significant changes, you should identify the skills and experiences you already have that can be transferred to the tech industry. This includes both business and soft skills, as there are a variety of non-technical roles within the tech industry that can use your existing skills.

Once you clearly understand your skills and experience, you should research the different types of companies and organizations within the tech industry to see which ones align with your interests and goals. This can include startups, established tech companies, and even nonprofits that use technology to achieve their missions.

Build a network of connections within the tech industry, as this can help you to learn about job opportunities, get advice from industry insiders, and build relationships with potential employers. You can start building your network by attending events and conferences, participating in online forums and social media groups, and reaching out to people who work in the tech industry.

Stay up-to-date with the latest developments and trends in the field. This can include reading industry publications and websites, attending workshops and training sessions, and taking courses and certifications to increase your knowledge and skills.

When applying for jobs in the tech industry, it is essential to tailor your resume and cover letter to the specific job you are applying for. This means highlighting your relevant skills and experiences and demonstrating how they make you a good fit for the position. You should also be prepared to answer questions related to the tech industry during job interviews, as many tech companies will test your knowledge and problem-solving skills as part of the hiring process.

Lastly, have a positive attitude and be willing to learn and grow. This includes being open to new experiences, taking on new challenges, and being flexible and adaptable to change. With the right mindset, determination, and preparation, you can successfully transition into the tech industry and build a rewarding career in this exciting and fast-paced field.

Don't miss out!

Visit the website below and you can sign up to receive emails whenever Adebola Sanni publishes a new book. There's no charge and no obligation.

https://books2read.com/r/B-A-KIGY-SFRIC

BOOKS 2 READ

Connecting independent readers to independent writers.

About the Author

Adebola Sanni is a Fintech Growth and Innovation Expert who has consulted for top international brands like Google, MTN, Shell Foundation, IFC World Bank, USAID. Adebola has multi-faceted skills which cut across diverse areas.

She is a pioneer in new product development and solutions designed to meet the demands of the digital age, with sound knowledge of e-commerce, multi-device payment, financial solutions, applications, and emerging new technologies. A coach and consultant on digital transformation, its applications and strategies for implementation.

Currently, Adebola is the Co-founder of ErrandGoC LLC, an organisation that helps financial institutions transition to a NeoBank within 24 hours. She is also a Director at Infibranches Technologies, a pioneer company that developed a product that takes financial & energy access to the last mile. She masterminds product roadmaps, strategy development, partnerships, building, managing, and motivating teams to work collaboratively to achieve the overall business growth objectives.

She has an excellent information technology background. As an In-depth experienced Managing Consultant, She has an analytical and tactical understanding of business needs, including integrating technological solutions to streamline processes, improve efficiency and drive revenue growth.

Adebola is an astute advocate of Financial Inclusivity. She currently mentors at Techstar, Women in Management, Business and Public Service (WIMBIZ) and Women in Africa (WIA Initiative); and is also a member of top associations in technology, a speaker and advocate for Energy access. She is recognised as a thought leader in technology along being a WomenTech Global Ambassador and a panelist for the Lagos Fintech Week event and a Masterclass speaker at the CommAvenue.

As a serial achiever, Adebola co-hosts webinars with Google to educate businesses on digital skills, remote working and other business values. Selected as part of the team for Digital Startup Accelerator by Forbes. Recognized by over 40 news outlets as a major contributor and leader in technology, financial inclusion and energy access space.

She holds a BSc in Computer Science from Covenant University and a Master's degree in Information Technology from the University of Lagos. She is a professional member of the Project Management Institute, International Institute of Business Analysis and of several professional bodies.